# Teaching Your Child about SEX

Terrance S. Drake, M.D.

Marvia Brown Drake

Deseret Book Company
Salt Lake City, Utah

Library of Congress Catalog Card Number 83-071726

ISBN 0-87579-256-1

Printed in the United States of America

10   9   8   7   6   5   4   3   2

# Contents

# Introduction

Where do babies come from? Why does it take a mom and dad to make a baby? Children are always asking questions. It's a natural part of growing up. Some questions we don't know how to answer. Others make us feel uncomfortable. How much do we say? When should we tell our children about the complete process of creating life?

This book was written to help parents who believe that sexuality should be taught within the home and within the context of the gospel of Jesus Christ, thus allowing parents to emphasize principles of sexuality that go far beyond the anatomy, physiology, and contraception taught in the public schools. The method presented here follows the natural process of sexual discovery that inevitably occurs as children pass through the stages of sexual maturation. Prepared parents can use the many "teaching moments" that frequently occur from earliest childhood through adolescence. In a natural and comfortable way, they can educate their children sexually and morally.

The real issue is not whether children should or

should not receive instruction in sexuality. The real issue is who will teach it. Children are continuously growing and changing, and their sexuality cannot be concealed, ignored, or avoided. Their questions will be answered, whether on the school yard, in the classroom, on television, or by sensitive parents who love them and want to share gospel principles with them.

The goals of this book are, first, to convince parents that they are fully qualified and best suited to teach sexuality to their children, and second, to present a method to help them teach it early and naturally and from a gospel perspective.

# 1

# You Can Teach Your Children

Recently we were explaining to parents the importance of teaching sexuality in the home so that proper emphasis on values and self-control could be given. On hearing this, one father said, "It's easy for you to do. You're a doctor!" Many people believe that only someone with special training or a medical background is qualified to instruct in this sensitive area. Unfortunately, this common misconception is held by many parents and educators.

## Technical Knowledge

Just how much specific, technical physiology, anatomy, and reproductive science must parents understand to effectively teach sexuality to children? Some educators claim that a detailed knowledge of male and female physiology is mandatory. We do not believe this to be the case. In fact, all of the necessary facts about male sexuality can be summarized as follows:

Male genital organs include the penis, the scrotum, and the testicles. A boy notices from a very early age that his penis can get hard and enlarged. This is normal and is called an erection. It simply means that extra blood is filling the penis. The erection serves a very important purpose later in life when the young man wants to become a father.

The testicles have two functions. Both become operative between the ages of ten and fourteen. The first function is the production of the male hormone, testosterone, which causes increased height and muscle, a voice change, the growth of body hair, and many other subtle changes of early manhood. The second function of the testicles is to produce sperm. These are special cells that, when combined with a woman's egg, can lead to the development of a new human being.

Some boys have sexual dreams during which they release sperm cells automatically during sleep. This is normal, and need not be a source of worry.

This is all the basic information parents need to instruct children about male sexuality. Most parents already know this material. Of course, there are many details of reproductive physiology and endocrinology that are not even mentioned here, but these are not essential in teaching sexuality to children.

The basic facts of female sexuality are equally simple and direct:

The female genital organs include the vagina, the uterus, and the ovaries. The ovaries are similar to the male testicles. Only the vagina can be seen from the outside.

Between the ages of nine to thirteen a girl begins to experience sexual change. This is the result of her ovaries starting to produce a hormone called estrogen, the female hormone, which causes increased height, breast development, body hair, and many other subtle changes of early womanhood.

As the ovaries continue to function a girl will notice the onset of menstruation. This is when blood passes from the uterus and out the vagina each month. It is normal and indicates that the reproductive organs are functioning properly. It is also a sign that the young woman is producing an egg, which is released from her ovaries. This egg is called an ovum, and if it comes in contact with sperm, a pregnancy can result, with the subsequent growth of a baby within the girl's uterus.

Again, this is all the information parents need to instruct their children about female sexuality. Most parents already know this information and can teach it to their children.

## Why You Are the Best Teacher

There are several reasons parents are best suited to teach their children about sexuality. The first is availability. No other person spends more time with a child than the child's mother and father. Thus, parents can teach when questions first come up. No other people share with children the intimacy of such events as bath time, potty training, menstruation, and so on. Prepared parents sensitive to the process of teaching about sexuality are far superior to a schoolteacher exposed to children for only a few hours in a formal setting.

Also, parents share with their children common values and love and concern. Sexuality cannot and should not be separated from morality. No one is better qualified to teach chastity, self-control, and moral conduct than parents. As parents answer their children's earliest questions about sexuality or childbirth, they can emphasize the sacred nature of reproduction and the body. These important lessons could not be learned in the classroom with teachers who have only a casual acquaintance with the children and who may not share the values of the children and their parents.

## Single Parents

Where death or divorce leaves a parent alone, or where one parent for one reason or another will not participate in the sexual education of the children, the responsibility for that education will have to be borne primarily by the one parent.

The single parent can use all aspects of the method outlined in this book. Some difficulty may be encountered by a mother with a teenage son or a father with a teenage daughter, and in these instances, the single parent may need to rely heavily on books written for teenagers.

The single parent may also get help from a close family friend who shares common ideals. A father may ask a Laurel leader to talk with his teenage daughter, a mother may call on a bishop, home teacher, or scoutmaster to talk with her teenage son. Still, teaching a child about sex is a continual process, and it is really the parent's responsibility.

Regardless of the resources you use, you *can* teach your children everything they need to know about sexuality. You are the most qualified, sensitive educator that your child could have.

# 2

# How *Not* to
# Teach Your Children

Parents commonly use one of three methods to teach sexuality to children. Although each method has some merit, they all share one major deficiency—they fail to view sexuality as something that should be taught from the child's earliest discovery of sexuality to young adulthood.

## Method One: Wait and Worry

Parents who use this method typically think something like this: "Mary is a mature young lady, well adjusted; when she has questions about sex, she'll ask them."

"Wait and worry" is the most common of the three methods. Parents who use it may think about teaching sexuality to their children from time to time, but never get around to it. The parents often discuss the matter alone, however:

Mother:      Tom, Mary started menstruating last month. Don't you think it's about time for you to have a father-daughter talk with her?

Father:     Has she asked any questions yet? I really think when she's ready she'll ask us. Don't you?

The "wait and worry" parents let year after year slip away without any direct communication with their children about sexuality. To their surprise, their children seem not to care very much. As a child approaches his early teens and his pubertal changes are becoming obvious, any questions he wants to ask about sex cease. Sexuality has now become a personal matter, since the child is beginning to experience his own sexual awakening. Communication naturally becomes more difficult between parents and children during these years. The parents take some comfort in the fact that special talks and classes are held in church stressing chastity. As the dating age approaches, the "wait and worry" parents may attempt their first and only direct communication on sexuality:

Father:     Bob, you'll be sixteen next month. You'll be able to start dating.

Son:        Yeah, and I'll finally get my driver's license. Boy, I hope I can use the Dodge for some of the special activities. Do you think that will be okay?

Father:     Probably. Bob, with dating come very important responsibilities, especially to the young ladies you will be dating. Young men your age can get strong urges, and these need to be controlled . . . Do you know what I'm talking about?

Son:        Sure, you're talking about sex. I know all about that stuff. Listen, Dad, I've got to run. Could we talk about this later?

This father may be relieved by Bob's statement that he knew "all about that stuff." The father might think to himself, "What a smart young man! There was nothing to it. I knew he was well adjusted." Although this father may be left with a vague uneasiness over when and how the young man gathered his information on sex, he is, nevertheless, relieved.

"Wait and worry" parents don't realize that the sexual education of their children will take place with or without them. In most instances, the children's questions will be answered on the school yard, by a friend, or in the classroom. Sometimes, however, a young man or woman will reach adulthood or marriage with inadequate knowledge about sex and may have significant social and marital problems. These instances are rare, though. Most children seek and find answers to their questions about the changes they see in their bodies.

Parents who use the "wait and worry" method forfeit all control over how, when, and in what context their children learn about sexuality. They lose the opportunity to put sexuality into a perspective that emphasizes the gospel principles of morality, responsibility, self-mastery, and so on. And the child loses the parents' loving counsel and feelings about this important aspect of life.

## Method Two: The Big Night
The "big night" approach goes something like this:

Father:     Margerie, you turned thirteen last month. Tonight your mother is going to have a special talk with you about an important subject.

Daughter:   I've been invited to Joyce's for the night. Couldn't we do it some other time?

Father:    Well, maybe, but you need to have this talk. Talk to your mother about when it would be best, okay?

The parent who chooses this method has made the incorrect assumption that sexual education is an isolated event to be scheduled because a certain age or developmental stage such as starting high school, menstruation, or dating has been reached. This is clearly the most traumatic method for the parents. They have probably never directly discussed anatomy or sexuality with their child prior to the "big night" and will probably never discuss it with them again.

The parent who chooses this method uses such terms as *penis, vagina, uterus, intercourse,* and so on in an awkward and unnatural way with the child. Since only one night has been set aside, the child may be preoccupied with a television show he's missing, a bike ride that has been delayed, or some other activity.

One mother who used this approach reported that several months after her one-and-only talk with her fourteen-year-old daughter on the "facts of life," she asked her daughter if she remembered the talk and the things they discussed. The girl was unable to remember even having the talk with her mother. The mother was surprised and disappointed, since she had gone through many nervous moments getting ready for the "big night." In retrospect, it was obvious that her daughter had not only failed to learn the principles the mother had "taught," but she could not even remember the night!

The failure of this method is two-fold. First, it fails to recognize that sexuality is discovered and learned over many years, not just in one night. Second, it fails to match the teaching with moments when the child asks questions and is receptive to learning. These "teaching moments" occur again and again during childhood, and the prepared parent should use them to teach little by little and precept upon precept the many aspects of human sexuality.

## Method Three: "Here, read this"

A parent using this method says something like this:

Father:     Tom, I've left a book on the dresser in your bedroom. Now that you're twelve it's important for you to read and understand the facts of life the book discusses. I want you to read it, okay?

Son:        Sure.

Some parents who choose this method will say nothing. They will simply leave the book in a conspicuous place and assume the child will understand the unspoken message of the book's importance. To be sure, many books about sexuality have been written for children. Some are vague and unclear, others are direct, insensitive, and crude. Of course, a number of excellent books are available. Even when a parent chooses one of the better books on sexuality for a child to read, they make two assumptions that may not be true. First, they assume the child will read and understand the book. Second, they assume the book contains all the principles of sexuality and morality they want their child to learn.

Of the three methods discussed in this chapter, this method may be the most useful. If parents supplement their own comments on sexuality with books on this subject written for children, the child may effectively learn what he needs to know. Such teaching may begin in early childhood, since well-written books are available for preschoolers. Some of these books offer excellent and sensitive illustrations. These books can often be found in the library as well as in LDS bookstores. One excellent three-volume series written by Glen C. Griffin, M.D., is published through Deseret Book.

However, if parents do not supplement books with their own insights, this method may be as ineffective as the two methods previously described.

In general, these three methods are not adequate to teach children about sexuality.

3

# The Best Way to Teach

The first step in teaching your children about sexuality is to accept the fact that it is okay to talk about sexuality with them and with each other. Sexuality is not some terrible weakness or evil condition afflicted upon men and women to torment or tempt them. Sexuality was divinely created for procreation and for the very important purpose of creating a strong and lasting bond between a man and a woman, a bond so strong that they could become "one flesh." It is as important for our children to understand sexuality as it is for them to understand the principles of honesty and repentance. Most Latter-day Saint parents agree that their children should be taught sexuality within the context of the gospel, but they usually have no idea how to do it. They are not sure what words to use or when and how to teach.

In this chapter we will outline a simple, natural method for teaching sexuality in the home. If this teaching is started early in the child's life, it will establish parents as a reliable source of accurate answers to the child's questions about this most interesting subject. It will also permit the parents to emphasize such gospel principles as chastity, self-mastery, and responsibility.

Consider the following ways parents might respond to teaching opportunities.

Example one: A mother notices that her four-year-old son is pulling curiously at his penis after bathtime.

Response 1: Don't do that! It isn't nice.

Response 2: Sometimes it feels good to touch your penis like that, doesn't it? That's because it's a very special part of your body. Since it's so special, you shouldn't touch or pull at it like you're doing. It's also very private, so let's get some pants on right after bathtime, okay?

Example two: A seven-year-old asks, "How did a baby get into Mrs. Walker's stomach?"

Response 1: You'll learn about that later when you're a little older. Now, run out and play."

Response 2: A small cell has started to grow inside Mrs. Walker's uterus. During the next nine months it will grow from the size of a grain of sand to a newborn baby. Having a baby is one of the most beautiful times in a woman's life.

Example three: The seven-year-old persists, "But what made the egg grow? How did it start?"

Response 1: I told you to go outside and play. You're asking questions that you shouldn't. Now, here's a cookie, and please go.

Response 2: You seem very interested in Mrs. Walker's pregnancy. I've got a book that we can look at together. It shows how a seed from a man joins an egg from a woman to start making a baby. Maybe later after I'm through with my work we can sit down and look at it, okay?

In each of the above examples, the person giving the second response was sensitive to the teaching moment that had arisen. In example 1, the parent giving the first response gave a negative message to the child about the genital area: It isn't nice—it shouldn't be touched or wondered about! In the second response of this example, the parent used simple and direct language to reinforce the correct anatomic term, to teach that the genital area is special, and to introduce the principle of modesty.

In the second and third examples, the parent giving the first response did not want to discuss the simple facts of human reproduction. The parent was, no doubt, unprepared. The parent also failed to realize that most seven-year-olds are very curious—they want facts and more facts. Although a cookie may have worked as a temporary distraction, the child's curiosity was no doubt heightened by the parent's reaction. Probably, the child's reaction was: "Something about having babies is a secret my parents won't tell me. I wonder who will?"

The second responses in the second and third examples were direct and accurate. Note that the parent did not launch into a full anatomic explanation when the child asked how the baby got into Mrs. Walker's stomach. When the child persisted, the parent gave more factual information and set up an opportunity to discuss the matter in greater detail with a good supplement. The child left confident that his parent was a source of accurate information and that complete answers to his questions would be available with no more than a simple request.

The basic principles of the method used by the parents giving the second responses can be summarized as follows:

*1. Be prepared.*   From earliest childhood, your children will give you opportunities to teach about sexuality in a natural setting. Have in your home several books on the subject written for children. Rehearse by yourself or with your spouse simple and direct ways to explain the various aspects of human sexuality (childbirth, intercourse, fetal growth, and so on). (Many examples of ways to do this will be presented in chapters 4, 5, and 6.)

*2. Be honest and direct.*   Give direct and anatomically correct answers. You may not be comfortable saying such words as *penis, vagina, testicle,* and so on, but the sooner you introduce these terms to your child, the easier it will be to present more advanced concepts as the child grows. Never distort simple truths with made-up names or fantasies to explain such things as childbirth or sexual intercourse.

*3. Be sensitive.*   Be sensitive to the teaching moment presented. Does the child want a complete answer? Is the time and place right? Would a partial answer and a promise to discuss it later be best? You should, in general, answer as much of the child's question as will satisfy him. The amount you answer will vary from a simple sentence to a thirty-minute detailed discussion. This will depend on the age of the child and the conditions under which the question is asked.

*4. Be observant.*   The child may not always create the teaching moment with a question. In the example above, the prepared parent used the common occurrence of genital play in a four-year-old to introduce the principle of modesty and the special nature of the sexual organs. Many such teaching moments will present themselves, and the observant parent will take the opportunity to teach a principle. (Further examples of how to do this will be given in chapter 4.)

*5. Be careful.* Your attitudes can teach your children much about sexuality. The pregnant mother who constantly complains about how sick she feels when she is pregnant may convey a negative message to her daughter about this special time in a woman's life. The father who in frustration yells at his son, "If you don't stop that, you're going to get some girl pregnant!" may be giving his boy the incorrect message that his major concern is avoiding an unwanted pregnancy with no apparent concern for moral behavior.

*6. Be diligent.* A parent's diligence should continue into young adulthood. The months of serious courtship and even the weeks after engagement are often the most difficult for a young man or woman. It is just as important to give loving and direct counsel at this time as when the child was young. A parent might say something like this:"Bev, we're so happy about your engagement. A temple wedding in June! What more could a mother ask for? Now, my dear daughter, the next four months may be the most difficult for you and Bruce. Your physical attraction will grow and grow. I understand this, but remember that sexual contact is beautiful and right only when you are married. Then and only then will it bring you joy instead of sorrow and regret."

Such timely counsel might prevent sin and sorrow for the young couple.

These principles can be effectively applied only if parents realize that their children are passing through specific developmental stages and that the same question may need a very different "correct" answer based on a child's development. These stages are preschool (ages two through five), prepubertal (ages six through ten), pubertal (ages eleven through fifteen), adolescent (ages sixteen through eighteen), and young adulthood (ages nineteen through twenty-five). The age range for each stage is only approximate and may vary from child to child. The stages are explained below.

## Preschool

These are the years when a child is in close continual contact with his parents. Language skills develop during this period, and by age five the child is curious and talkative. These are the years of learning to correctly name objects and distinguish between different colors and shapes. For most children, these are the best years to introduce the correct anatomic names for the male and female genital organs. Also during these early years, the special and sacred nature of sexual differences between boys and girls can be introduced. This is also the time to teach the principles of modesty, privacy, and respect for others.

The child has not yet been exposed to other children who will introduce the idea that sexual matters are "dirty" and "nasty," so now is the best time to give the child a positive understanding about boy and girl sex differences and emphasize that those who make fun of such things are wrong. In many ways, these first three years are the most important in establishing a base upon which future discussions can be built.

## Prepubertal

During this stage, a child develops an immense curiosity and is eager to learn. *How* and *why* questions are the most important to these children, so this stage presents the best opportunity to teach a child the functional facts about sexuality: where babies come from, how they start growing, why babies breast-feed, what menstruation is, and so on.

These are important social years. The child will

develop close friends, and his peer group will become very important. Children this age want to be liked by their friends, to be a part of the gang, which includes doing the same things, wearing the same clothes, and using the same vocabulary as their friends. Parents need to be aware of the influence the peer group has on their children. Friends might tell jokes or use language that makes fun of sexuality. Other children will emphasize the "secret" and "dirty" nature of things.

A child learns to choose between right and wrong during this stage. Parents need to make sure their children are taught the correct facts about sexuality with a strong emphasis on their special and sacred nature. It would not be inappropriate for a nine-year-old to have a simple and clear understanding of the process of human reproduction and its important role in God's plan. This affords excellent preparation for the child as he enters his years of pubertal change and sexual awakening.

## Pubertal

No period in a child's life is filled with more change than the years of puberty. The child will grow four to five inches within a few months, the voice will change, body hair will appear, breasts will develop, and the sexual organs will become functional. During these years the child may experience great insecurity over how he or she looks. Communication between parents and children may become more difficult. Severe mood swings from total happiness to deepest depression may occur with regularity.

When a child reaches this period, the time for teaching accurate and positive facts about sexuality has passed. Sexuality has now become very personal, since the child can see and feel it in himself. These are the years to teach responsibility about sexuality. The concept of masturbation should be brought up in a sensitive and direct way. (See chapter 6.) Parents must communicate understanding for what a child is experiencing and reassurance that a child's bodily changes are normal and right. The beautiful and sacred nature of sexuality needs to be emphasized within the context of the law of chastity. This provides an excellent foundation for the dating years that will soon follow.

## Adolescence

These are the dating years. For most young people, sexual maturation is almost complete. Attraction for the opposite sex is now much stronger. This is the time for parents to give specific, personal counsel. Parents should share their feelings with their adolescent children about the beauty and joy of love and sexuality within the confines of a temple marriage. This is a good time for direct, plain talk about the consequences of immoral behavior. Venereal disease and abortion can be discussed, not as a scare tactic but as a way to explain the great tragedy that accompanies immorality. This is the time to define exactly what is expected of a child if he is to go on a mission or enter the temple. These young people are responsive to direct, specific talk about necking and petting and how to avoid them while dating.

Parents must avoid constant badgering and show understanding and loving concern for their child's happiness.

## Young Adulthood

These are the years of courtship and marriage. It is important for parents to realize that during these years young men and women may feel their most intense sexual desires. Direct and loving counsel may still be appropriate months, weeks, and even days before a temple marriage to avoid sorrow and guilt in later years.

## *Summary*

From their earliest years, children learn about sexuality. They begin by learning the simple distinction between boys and girls (preschool) and progress to an intense interest about how reproduction occurs (prepuberty). Then comes children's own sexual awakening and physical change (puberty), followed by dating (adolescence) and finally by courtship and marriage (young adulthood).

Parents need to parallel this natural progression with honest and direct teaching appropriate to the specific stage of a child's development. They should always emphasize the sacred nature of sexuality, even when answering questions of the youngest child.

As parents teach using this method, their children will learn that the home is their best source of accurate information. In addition, the direct communication between parents and children on this special subject can strengthen their relationship at each stage of development.

# 4

# When to Teach

What is a teaching moment? It is a point in time when the child is teachable, when all of the conditions are right to allow a principle or concept to be taught in an easy and natural way. One of the most obvious teaching moments a parent experiences is when a child asks a question. Questions about sexuality are most likely to occur during the prepubertal years. This provides parents with many rich opportunities to teach the facts of human sexuality during this stage.

The way a parent answers a child's earliest questions about sexuality will usually determine whether future questions will follow.

A six-year-old asks, "Mom, why does my penis get hard like this?"

Response 1:  Don't worry about that, it's nothing. Now get some pants on!

Response 2:  That's called an erection. It's very normal and simply means that extra blood is inside your penis. It will be important later when you're a man and are ready to be a father.

If the parent answers the child's first questions about sexuality in an evasive or negative way, the child will quickly determine that this subject is something his parents won't talk about, something secretive that makes them nervous. This might support the school-yard talk that sexual matters are dirty and nasty, and he may be reluctant to talk about them ever again.

In the second response, the parent gave a simple and correct answer to the child's question. She introduced the concept that the erect penis is necessary for fatherhood. The six-year-old may be completely satisfied with this answer, or he may persist in his questioning: "How does it help me be a father?"

Response:     After a boy is thirteen or fourteen, he develops special seeds, called sperm, that help make a baby grow inside its mother. These seeds can only leave a man's body through the penis when it is erect. That's why it will be important later on when you're ready to be a father.

The child will probably be satisfied with this second response. If his questions continue, then more direct information should be given. As the child runs off to busy himself with some other activity, he understands basic concepts that will be important as he has future questions or as teaching moments present themselves.

All of the times to teach sexuality do not begin with a child's questions. Some children are shy and ask very few questions. Others may already have the misconception that sexual matters are evil and dirty and that they should not ask questions about them. Many other times during a child's development can be used to teach about sexuality. Some of these are discussed below.

## *Toilet Training*

This time is limited to the early preschool years and provides a natural and repetitive setting to teach anatomy, stress proper hygiene, and teach modesty.

## *Bath Time*

Often two or even three children will bathe together. This happens most often during the preschool and early prepubertal years. This affords an excellent opportunity to teach anatomy and point out genital differences between boys and girls.

## *Pregnancy*

The period when a child's mother or relative or even a pet is pregnant is often a good time to teach many of the basic concepts of human reproduction. Different aspects of human sexuality will be taught depending on the child's stage of development. Several examples follow:

Example 1: A three-year-old boy is staring at his pregnant mother's stomach.

Son:  Mommy, your tummy is so big.
Mother:  There is a beautiful new baby growing inside my uterus. Soon you'll be able to see and hold the baby. This is a very special time for our family, isn't it?

Example 2: A seven-year-old is staring at his pregnant mother as she elevates her feet after sitting down.

Mother:  Come here, Brad. Put your hand right here and you can feel the baby move.
Son:  How does the baby eat inside of you, Mom?
Mother:  He gets all of the food right from my body. It enters through his belly-button. That will all stop after he is born.

Example 3. A ten-year-old boy watches as his pregnant mother practices breathing exercises. His mother creates a teaching opportunity by asking a question: "Bobby, do you know why I practice breathing this way?"

| | |
|---|---|
| Son: | No. |
| Mother: | Having a baby can be painful. These breathing exercises help me relax my muscles to make it easier. |
| Son: | You mean it hurts to have a baby? Where does it come out? |
| Mother: | It does hurt some. There is a special opening in a woman. We've talked about it before. It's called the vagina. This stretches open, and the baby comes out through it. |
| Son: | Aaron said his mother had their baby through her stomach. |
| Mother: | Mrs. Bailey had an operation called a cesarean section. When the baby can't safely come through the vagina, the doctor can make a hole in the mother's stomach and take the baby out. |
| Son: | That's neat. |

Example 4: A thirteen-year-old daughter says to her pregnant mother, "Mom, your breasts are getting so big. How come?"

| | |
|---|---|
| Mother: | They have grown, you're right. That's so they can provide all the milk the baby will need after he is born. |
| Daughter: | Do you have to breast-feed? Janet's mother gives their new baby a bottle. |
| Mother: | No, I don't have to breast-feed. A bottle will do just fine. I like to breast-feed my babies because it makes me feel very close to them. Motherhood is a beautiful time, Kay. It's something to prepare for. |

## Breast-Feeding

Breast-feeding provides an excellent opportunity to teach children about this important sex difference between men and women. It allows mothers and fathers to emphasize the beautiful and sacred nature of the female breast.

Example: A father sees his nine-year-old son watching his mother breast-feed their new baby.

Father:   Brad, there is nothing more beautiful than a mother nursing her baby. That's the real purpose of the female breast. No matter how nasty or dirty your friends at school may try to make it seem, the breast serves a beautiful and important purpose. People who make fun of such things are wrong.

## Menstruation

Sometimes a child will find a tampon in the toilet, blood on his mother's underclothing, or a used sanitary napkin. Because bleeding usually means that someone is hurt, the child may be frightened and will need confident reassurance from the parent.

Example 1: A three-year-old sees a tampon in the toilet.

Daughter:   Mommy, what's that?
Mother:   It's a tampon. That blood is normal and simply means that mommy is menstruating. I am not hurt, and everything is okay.

Example 2: A seven-year-old finds undergarments with bloodstains in the laundry room.

Son:   Mother, there's blood on your clothes. What happened?

| Mother: | Nothing happened, Neil. I'm fine. That blood is normal and is called menstruation. |
| Son: | Why did you bleed? Where did it come from? |
| Mother: | It comes from a special organ inside me called the uterus. Blood comes out of it each month and is a sign that I'm not pregnant. It's normal and is supposed to be that way. |
| Son: | I don't get it. Why do you bleed? |
| Mother: | You seem very interested in this. I have a book that will help explain it. Would you like to look at it with me? |
| Son: | Sure. |

Example 3: A ten-year-old girl asks her mother, "Dana's sister started her period. She says it happens to every girl. What is a period?"

| Mother: | Dana's right. Every girl will have periods. Another name for a period is *menstruation*. This is when blood passes through the vagina each month for about four or five days. It's one of the first signs that a girl is becoming a woman. You don't need to worry about it. It is normal. |
| Daughter: | When will it happen to me? |
| Mother: | Probably when you are twelve or thirteen. |
| Daughter: | Does it hurt? |
| Mother: | Not usually. There may be some mild cramps for the first day or so, but that's all. |
| Daughter: | Why does it happen? |
| Mother: | The blood comes from the uterus. That is the special organ where babies grow. Each month the uterus gets ready for a baby. If |

one does not start growing, the woman bleeds and then the preparation begins again.

This may naturally lead to further questions:

Daughter: What starts the baby growing?

Mother: A seed from a man must enter the woman's uterus and combine with the cell that may become a baby. Only then will a baby start to grow.

Daughter: You mean Dana's sister could get pregnant? She's only fourteen.

Mother: Yes, she could. She's not ready for pregnancy, as you point out. But if she had sexual intercourse with a young man, she could get pregnant. When this happens to a young girl before marriage it brings great problems and sorrow. It is also one of the most serious sins a boy and girl can commit. Sexual intercourse is only for a husband and wife who have been properly married. It is a sacred power Heavenly Father has given us. If it is used properly, it can bring us great happiness and joy.

## Child Uses a Bad Word

Example 1: A seven-year-old shocks his parents while watching television with them: Oh, look, they're hugging. Are they going to "hump," Dad?

Father: Where did you hear that word, Son?

Son: Mark told me that when men and women loved each other, they humped.

Father: Do you know what that means?

Son: Not really. *(The child may also give a correct*

|          | *answer or incorrect answer, but the parent's response should be the same.)* |
|----------|-----------------------------------------------|
| Father:  | That's a very bad word, Son. It makes fun of something that is sacred and special. Some kids try to make it seem dirty or nasty, but they're wrong. It is special and good, and should not be made fun of. |
| Son:     | What does it mean, Dad? |
| Father:  | Let's turn the television off and we can talk about it, okay?. |
| Son:     | Sure. |
| Father:  | The closest physical contact a man and woman can have is called sexual intercourse. It is when the man holds the woman very close and puts his penis into her vagina. This is the only way the seed from the man can enter the woman so that a baby can be born. |
|          | Having babies is a special, sacred power Heavenly Father has given us. It should be used only between husband and wife. Sometimes people make fun of this power. They make it seem dirty. Many boys and girls and men and women have sexual intercourse before they are married. This is wrong. It is a great sin. It brings unhappiness and sorrow into many lives when it is used in this way. |
|          | On the other hand, when it's done between a loving husband and wife, it is beautiful and can deepen their love. Do you understand why we shouldn't make fun of it? |
| Son:     | Yeah, and thanks, Dad. |

Parents must realize that experiences like these occur in every home and that the way they handle them will determine to a great extent the child's attitudes about sexuality. Parents must be prepared for, not shocked by, a child's sudden questions. Giving forthright answers that emphasize the sacred nature of sexuality is important.

Teaching moments may begin with a child's question or with a family experience. These are the perfect times to teach about sexuality. If parents start this teaching early, new concepts will be easier to teach because any instruction will build upon vocabulary and truths taught in earlier years.

# 5

# Teaching Principles as Well as Facts

The major advantage of having parents teach their children about sexuality is that they can do so within the context of gospel principles. A balance between facts and principles is important in answering even the youngest child's questions. Sex education programs in the schools purposely avoid teaching values of any kind. The following example illustrates this kind of teaching:

Daughter:    How do babies get inside a mother?
Mother:       The baby starts growing inside the mother's uterus. This is the result of a process called sexual intercourse. Sperm from the man fertilizes an egg within the mother and the baby's growth begins.

This answer is physiologically correct, but it gives no moral perspective to the concept being taught. It suggests neither a positive nor a negative attitude toward reproduction.

An equally ineffective way to answer the child's question would be to teach only principles and avoid the facts. Here is an example of this kind of teaching:

Daughter:    How do babies get inside a mother?

Mother:  The baby starts growing because of the deep love the parents share for each other. It is one of God's great gifts to us. It is a blessing and great responsibility, something to prepare for.

In this case, the child certainly gets the message that something about having babies is very special. She can sense her mother's sincerity, but her question was not really answered. She is left puzzling over the mechanics of how conception takes place.

With a little practice, parents can learn to blend facts with principles to satisfy the child's curiosity and at the same time emphasize the sacred nature of reproduction. Here is an example of how this might be done:

Son:  How do babies get inside a mother?

Mother:  A seed from the father must join with a special cell in the mother to start the growth of the baby within the mother's uterus. It is the most special time in a mother and father's life. It strengthens their love and lets them share with God the miracle of giving life.

Many gospel principles can be easily and naturally integrated into teaching the basic facts about sexuality. Following are several of these principles with examples of how they might be used to help teach children about reproduction.

## *Principle: The Importance of the Family*

Example 1: A three-year-old stares at his pregnant mother as she dresses.

Mother:  Soon we will have a little brother or sister for you to play with. The baby is growing in a special place inside me. That's why my tummy is getting bigger. Daddy and you and I are a family. When the new baby comes, he will be part of our family too. Families are very special.

Example 2: A nine-year-old is complaining about his allowance.

Son:
Derek gets everything. There are only two kids in his family, and he gets ten dollars a week allowance. Why do we have so many kids? Derek says there are ways to stop having kids!

Mother:
There are many ways that parents can choose to prevent having children. Your dad and I are happy to have all of our seven children. Each helps make our family complete. We're very happy we didn't stop after just two.

Such an answer may lead to questions about contraception. These questions should be answered directly and honestly:

Mother:
Whenever the parents do anything that prevents the father's seed from reaching the special cell within the mother, a pregnancy is prevented. There are many ways this can be done. Father and I don't think that these methods should be used just to keep our family small so we can have more money. This is selfish and never brings happiness.

## Principle: The Miracle of Creating Life.

Example 1: A five-year-old is staring at her new baby brother.

Mother:     Jennifer, isn't Brian a beautiful baby? Look at his perfect little hands and feet. Isn't it a miracle that such a perfect baby came from inside me? This is one of God's greatest gifts to a woman to make her happy.

Example 2: An eleven-year-old hears his father talking about their new baby.

Father:     Well, he's got your eyes, honey, but he definitely has my nose. He's a good-looking boy!

Son:        How can he have Mom's eyes and your nose? I don't get it.

Father:     You know, son, that it takes a seed or sperm from a father to join with a cell or ovum in a mother to start the growth of a baby. We've talked about that before. Well, on the seed from me are all of my traits, like my hair color, the shape of my nose and face, and so on. On the cell from Mother are all of her traits. These are called genes. Each new baby has some of the father's and some of the mother's traits. This is the way Heavenly Father planned for a mother and father to share in the creation of a child.

## *Principle: Modesty*

Example 1: A mother sees her four-year-old running down the hall without any clothes after bath time.

Mother:     Shawn, you have no clothes on. There are very special parts of your body that you should keep covered after your bath is

over. Now, let me help you get some pa-
jamas on.

Example 2: A thirteen-year-old daughter in a de-
partment store is upset with her mother.

Daughter:     Why can't I buy a two-piece bathing suit?
              Every girl I know wears one. It isn't fair!
Mother:       Janet, I'm sorry we don't agree on this. You
              have a beautiful body. Certain parts of it
              are very special and private, and your
              father and I both feel that they should be
              covered properly when you wear a bathing
              suit. Now, let's try to find one that makes
              us both happy.

## *Principle: Difference between Men and Women*
Example 1: A four-year-old boy watches his
mother as she breast-feeds a new baby.

Son:          Can a boy feed a baby like that?
Mother:       No, boys do not develop breasts the way
              girls do. This is a special part of being a
              mother. Only girls get to do it. You're
              going to be a daddy. You will have many
              things to do with your baby when you're a
              dad, things like rocking the baby, reading
              him stories, feeding him cereal, teaching
              him to ride a bike, and many other such
              things.

Example 2: A ten-year-old surprises his parents by
asking, "What does it mean to be gay?"

Father:       What have you been told it means?
Son:          Craig says it's when one man kisses
              another.

| Father: | That is partly correct. Another name for *gay* is *homosexual*. Some men and even women get very mixed up. A gay person wants to date and even marry someone of the same sex, boy with boy, girl with girl. This is wrong, and it is a very serious sin. God created men and women different from each other so that they could be attracted to each other, marry in the temple, and have families. Homosexuals can't do this. |
|---|---|

## *Principle: Obedience*

Example: Father hugs his pregnant wife as their eleven-year-old watches.

| Father: | Your mother is carrying a beautiful baby inside her. This is a special time for us. Having children is one of life's greatest purposes. We are so happy we prepared for this time. |
|---|---|
| Son: | Jason's sister had an abortion. They were very sorry that she got pregnant. |
| Father: | That is so sad, and abortion is almost always a great sin. If a young man and woman prepare themselves for a temple marriage, their children will bring them great happiness. If they don't control their desires for each other, then the pregnancy will be unwanted and great sorrow will result. The ability to have children is one of God's greatest gifts to us. We must use it wisely. It is a great sin to violate this trust. |

Example 2: A sixteen-year-old priest says, "I think

Elder Banks is neat, Dad. Did you know he came from Canada?"

Father:    Elder Banks is a fine missionary. He is an excellent example of what every young man should be when he goes on a mission. It takes special preparation to serve a mission as faithfully as Elder Banks. When you are ready to serve, Bishop Jones will ask you many questions. Most of these questions will deal with your worthiness, especially how obedient you have been to the commandments.

Son:       Which commandments, Dad?

Father:    Well, paying tithing, keeping the Word of Wisdom, attending Church meetings, and others. One of the greatest stumbling blocks for many young men is the law of chastity. Some young men have had immoral sexual contact with young women or habitually masturbate. These things will prevent them from being able to serve a mission.

Son:       Why?

Father:    Basically, son, because the Lord will not be mocked, and it would be a mockery for a young man to serve a mission as a representative of Christ and yet violate these laws.

## *Principle: Self-Control*

Example 1: A fourteen-year-old says, "Diane's older sister is living with her boyfriend. Diane says they want to be sure they love each other before they get married."

Mother:       What do you think of that?

Daughter:     I guess it's wrong, since they are not married.

Mother:       Young men and women, even at your age, can be strongly attracted to each other. Sometimes they want to be together and have the same close sexual contact that they would have if they were married. That is what Diane's sister is really doing. This is wrong. It violates the law of chastity. Learning to control these desires and waiting to marry a special person in the temple brings joy and happiness.

Example 2: A father believes his fifteen-year-old son may need some counsel about masturbation.

Father:       Bob, let's sit down and talk a minute. You know, I can still remember what it was like to be fifteen. You're becoming a man and should be feeling sexual changes within your body. This is normal. Your physical development has now reached the point where your body can make sperm. This will be very important later when you want to become a father. Bob, this is one of the most sacred powers you have been given. It must be controlled, just as a person must learn to control anger or fear. Some boys make fun of these sexual feelings. Some think about sex and masturbate. This is a great mistake. Masturbation is false. It imitates the feeling a man will have during sexual intercourse with his wife. When these sexual desires are controlled and used only with a loving wife, they can bring great happiness. A misuse of this power brings only sorrow and guilt.

Such direct counsel assures the young man that his father understands what he is feeling. (The subject of masturbation will be considered further in chapter 6.)

Many additional principles could be emphasized. Some of these are responsibility to oneself and others, repentance, and eternal families.

Only parents can teach the many aspects of sexuality while emphasizing such gospel principles. This ensures that the child views sexuality not as something secretive and wrong, but as something special and sacred, and such teaching will guard against the child's learning a distorted or negative view of sexuality that could cause emotional and social problems. Such negative feelings about sexuality can affect even one's relationship with his spouse. But if gospel principles are taught with the basic facts about sexuality, the child will grow up with healthy, natural, and righteous attitudes about reproduction.

# 6

# Teaching Teenagers

Many parents with teenagers face a dilemma: they sense a need to give their teenagers some counsel about sexuality, but since they have never discussed the subject previously, they do not know how to bring it up. Communication between parents and children often becomes more difficult when the children become teenagers. This makes teaching teenagers more difficult than teaching young children. Most parents recognize that their teenagers have already acquired much basic information. Usually the parents are not certain where this information came from, and they are uncomfortable talking about it. Parents who want to discuss sexuality with their teenagers should remember three basic principles, each of which is discussed below:

## Principle 1: Use Personal Experiences Rather than Sermons

Example 1:

Mother:    Karen, we're told in the scriptures that no unclean thing can enter God's presence. It is vital that you keep yourself clean for that special day when you and your eternal partner are married in the temple. Then you will have true happiness.

Example 2:

Mother:   Karen, I can still remember what it was like to be fifteen. And I can still remember the name of my boyfriend. We thought we were very much in love. I remember that sometimes it was very hard for us not to just sit and kiss and kiss. I'm glad we didn't, and I'm glad that I saved all of those special moments of physical contact for your dad. That has made me very happy.

The message in both examples is the same, but the emphasis is very different. Example 1 is a sermon—unpleasant and preachy. Example 2 is an interesting personal experience that teaches with understanding. A typical teenage response to example 1 might be, "I know, I know! You don't have to worry, Mom."

A girl responding to example 2 might say, "What was his name? Did you really think you were in love?" or, "Did you really kiss him?" or, "What did you two do to keep from kissing all the time?"

With the responses to example 2, real communication has begun, providing an opportunity for the parent to teach self-control and chastity. Use personal examples. The more a child realizes that his parents understand what he is feeling, the more likely he is to listen to his parent's counsel.

## Principle 2: Be Direct and Honest
Example 1:

Mother:   Bev, you're like a beautiful white flower. If

you touch the delicate petal of a white flower, it turns brown and ugly. A flower is beautiful only when it is untarnished.

Example 2:

Mother:    Bev, your breast area is a very special part of your body. Don't let a young man touch this area. This type of petting suggests to the young man that you want to have sex with him. Close physical contact like petting should be saved for your husband.

Example 3:

Father:    Jim, man has been given a great power. When this power is controlled, it brings great happiness. When it is misused, it brings sorrow and regret. Always control the power within you.

Example 4:

Father:    Jim, many young men start dating with an eye to see how far they can go with a girl. Each date they try harder and harder to touch a young woman's breast or genital area. Petting is wrong. Such close physical contact should be saved for your wife. Then it will be special and beautiful. Under other conditions it brings guilt and sorrow.

Examples 1 and 3 are vague and abstract. Example 1 is also misleading, suggesting that sex is tarnishing even after marriage. Although the parents in these examples meant well, they were so general that their teenagers may have had no idea at all what they were talking about.

In examples 2 and 4, the parents gave direct, clear, helpful counsel. A young person receiving such counsel is apt to listen to and ponder the message. Teenagers are much more likely to respond to directness than to the abstract counsel sometimes given even by sincere parents.

## *Principle 3: Be Positive and Supportive*

Some teenagers have already gone too far. They habitually engage in heavy petting, and although they may feel some guilt and regret, they are uncertain about how to change things or if they can still repent. The worst message such a youth could get from his parents would be: "You're no good!" "You're a tramp." "I give up on you!" "You'll never change." Always be positive and supportive.

Example 1: A girl has just come home quite late from a date, something she has been doing quite regularly.

Father:   Jean, I believe you and Daryl have been touching each other's bodies where you shouldn't. I suspect that he has been touching your breast and genital area and that you have been touching his genitals. Am I right?

Daughter:  I guess so.

Father:   Believe me when I tell you that I understand how strong your attraction for each other is, but what you are doing is wrong. It will not make you happy, and right now, tonight, you should decide that it is finished. I know you can do it. Talk to Daryl. Find out if your relationship is deeper than just this physical involvement with each other. If it isn't, then your relationship is shallow and empty. Heavy petting like you have been doing will bring you only sorrow. I know you can stop it, and I know you will be happy with yourself when you do.

Such directness will register with a teenager. It offers hope and support. If the youth has transgressed to the point of sexual intercourse, then it is important to involve the bishop. He can make repentance possible and much easier. The bishop should also help a young person overcome petting. He can be of great help in overcoming masturbation as well.

It is important that a parent never give up on or stop loving the child. Rejection, even in a moment of great disappointment and anger, makes setting the youth's life back in order difficult if not impossible. It is sometimes difficult for a parent not to feel anger and shame, but these emotions need to be tempered with understanding and love.

Example 2: A mother discovers her twelve-year-old son reading a pornographic magazine.

Response 1:  You bum! Get that trash out of my house! I never want to see you reading anything like that again.

Response 2:  Darin, I am very upset to find you reading pornography. Such magazines make light of the sacredness of female sexuality. They are wrong because they artificially give you feelings that you should save for your wife. They also present false ideas about what sex between a loving husband and wife is like. You are far too fine a young man to be wasting your time with pornography. We have excellent books on female anatomy if you have any questions about it. Don't lower your standards to look at such magazines.

The mother giving the first response may have seriously hurt her relationship with her son. It would have been far better for her to express her disappointment while at the same time giving good reasons why her son should avoid pornography, as did the mother who gave the second response. Note that the second mother expressed confidence in her son and gave him something to live up to. Sometimes a parent will have very little warning about a situation like this, and his or her first reaction may determine if the relationship with the child is strengthened or destroyed.

Example 3: A father enters the living room and discovers his sixteen-year-old daughter "making out" with her boyfriend. The daughter's blouse is unbuttoned.

Response 1:  What's going on here? Tom, you get out of my house! And Bonnie, you get up to your room. You should be ashamed! Acting like some little tramp!

Here, the daughter is crying, upset, and embarrassed. The young man is out the door and running for his life. The father is red-faced and angry.

Response 2:  Bonnie, button your blouse. You two are making a big mistake. Tom, you should have respect for my daughter and keep your hands off her breasts. And Bonnie, you should respect yourself enough not to allow Tom to touch your breasts. I understand that you feel a strong attraction for each other, but you two should fill your time together with worthwhile activities instead of kissing and petting hour after hour. "Making out" will not bring you happiness. Such close physical contact is special and should be reserved for hus—band and wife. Then and only then can it bring joy.

Now, I'm going to leave you two to talk about this for the next twenty minutes. Decide right now if your relationship means more to you than just "making out." If it doesn't, then you are wasting your time together. If it does, then decide tonight that this business is finished.

You can be sure that the father giving the second response has the undivided attention of both teenagers. He used the moment to encourage communication between the couple, and he gave them important counsel. His relationship with his daughter has been strengthened by his controlled response. He may also have helped the young man set higher standards for dating.

Communication with teenagers can be the most difficult part of teaching sexuality. Using force and anger is ineffective and may damage your relationship with your teenager for many years to come. Giving direct and honest counsel, relating personal feelings and experiences, and controlling your anger will greatly strengthen your teaching. (Additional examples of direct answers to teenage questions about sexuality are given in the appendix.)

## Masturbation

Another important aspect of teaching teenagers about sexuality is helping them to avoid masturbation. Many young people have difficulty with this problem, but rarely do parents or Church leaders discuss it openly. Often the first time a young man is asked about masturbation is during his mission interview. Most young women are never counseled about it. No one is better equipped to give sensitive and loving counsel on this subject than the parent.

Rarely will it be necessary to discuss masturbation prior to puberty. Occasionally a prepubertal child will ask about masturbation because of something he has heard, and a simple and direct response to such questions should be given. With the dynamic physical changes during the pubertal years, many natural opportunities occur to introduce this concept. Parents need to be sensitive to the right moments.

Example: A father is watching his son shave.

Father:  Bob, it looks like you're going to be shaving every day pretty soon. Your body is changing quickly into that of a man. With this great physical change comes changes in your sexual development as well. Many young men think about sex a lot, and they create sexual fantasies in their minds and masturbate. This is wrong. Masturbation is a great imitator. It is false. It fools the body into feeling the same intense sexual feeling that a man should have only with his wife during intercourse. For some boys, it becomes a difficult habit to break. It is important to understand that these strong feelings are necessary and good in marriage but that they must be controlled. Just as a young man needs to learn to control his anger or fear, he must also control these sexual desires. It is wrong to masturbate. I want you to know this, and I also want you to know that I remember how hard it was to be fifteen. I know that controlling your sexual feelings is not easy, but I also know that you can do it, and avoiding masturbation will make you strong and happy, and will help you feel good about yourself.

The moments for such talks must be right. They must be private, and the youth's mind must not be distracted by other things. Timely counsel at these times by an understanding and loving parent may help the teenager resist the temptation to masturbate.

If the parent determines that the child has developed a chronic masturbation habit, then he should handle the problem just as he would any other bad habit. It is vital that the parent communicate understanding and support, not disgust and rejection. Here are some guidelines for helping young people avoid masturbation. The young person should:

1. Have a regular time for scripture reading and prayer.

2. Avoid long periods of idleness, lying awake in bed, sitting on the toilet, or taking long showers or baths.

3. Avoid all pornographic literature and movies. Such things can create feelings that lead to a desire to masturbate.

4. Talk openly with a parent about his progress in breaking his masturbation habit.

5. Avoid long periods of being alone.

6. Avoid depression and boredom. Developing interesting and wholesome hobbies is one way to do this.

7. Develop a good program of physical activity and exercise.

The great harm of masturbation is spiritual, not physical. There is not one bit of reliable medical information to suggest that masturbation is a health hazard. To use inaccurate "scare tactics" in counseling a teenager is wrong. He will determine that such information is wrong, and the parent will lose credibility.

Masturbation is wrong because it imitates the intense feelings God created for a husband and wife to have for each other. These feelings are not to be used for selfish moments of self-gratification but should be controlled and used to strengthen the bond of love between husband and wife. Masturbation treats lightly and casually that which is sacred. Perhaps most important, it is wrong because the Lord has said it is wrong.

Accuracy and directness in the earliest counseling about this difficult area will often be all that is necessary to prevent a problem that may negatively affect a young person well into adulthood. There is no "right age" or time to teach these principles. The child's own development will tell the prepared parent when the correct time has arrived. This will most often occur between the ages of twelve to fifteen for boys and eleven to fifteen for girls.

7

# It's Never Too Late
# to Teach

Many parents may think, "It's too late to properly
teach my children about sexuality. One of them is married, and two of them are in high school. I'm afraid I
missed my chance." This is a common attitude, and there
is some truth to what such parents feel. They have missed
the opportunity to direct the early sexual learning of
their children, and their teenagers have already learned
much about sexuality from classroom instruction as well
as school-yard talk. This does not mean, however, that
these parents have given up all influence on their children's future sexual education.

No matter how old a child is, it is never too late to talk
with him about this important subject. The observant
and motivated parent can accurately assess the level of
understanding a child has already achieved and then add
to or modify it as needed.

A parent may influence all aspects of sexual learning
when dealing with a preschooler. A parent beginning to
teach a prepubertal child will need to correct misinfor-
mation and emphasize a positive attitude toward sexuality. The pubertal youth needs reassurance and a strong

emphasis on the sacred and special nature of human sexuality. The adolescent needs directness and understanding. Parents should always share their sincere feelings with their children. It is all right for a parent simply to state, "I'm sorry I haven't talked with you before about these important matters."

Helping children establish high moral standards and positive attitudes about sexuality is one of a parent's most important responsibilities, and a parent should never hesitate to pray for help in finding the right teaching moment, recognizing what a child needs to know, or helping a child overcome problems related to sexuality. No one wants parents to succeed more than does the Lord. And no one can teach your children about sexuality more effectively and lovingly than you can.

# Appendix:
# Questions from Teenagers
# about Sex

Dr. Drake has answered many questions from teenagers about sex. Listed here are some of the most commonly asked questions and their answers.

Question:     What kind of defense can we use to control sexual feelings?

Answer:       Having sexual feelings or desires is normal. It is part of sexual maturation. A young person can, however, control how intense these feelings become. Don't dwell on sexual desires or feelings. Don't fill your mind with sexual fantasies. Occupy yourself with other activities. Do fifty pushups or jog a mile when you begin to have these feelings. Avoid lying awake in bed for long periods of time. Take quick showers and keep your time filled with activity. All of this will help you avoid masturbation.

Question:     What is petting?

Answer:       If a young man touches a girl's breasts or genital area, he is petting. If a girl touches a man's genitals, she is petting. Petting can be done through the clothing or under the clothing, but it is still petting. Petting can increase sexual intensity so greatly that it can become difficult for either partner to control. This can easily lead to sexual intercourse.

Question: How do you know that your sin is bad enough that you need to confess to your bishop?

Answer: If you have had sexual intercourse, you should confess it to your bishop. Doing this is essential for you to repent. You should see your bishop if you have been petting, and he can also help you repent of masturbating. You need to remember that you *can* receive complete forgiveness from the Lord. Sharing your problem with your bishop can be the first step to obtain this forgiveness.

Question: How does a person get a venereal disease?

Answer: Generally, venereal diseases are transmitted by sexual intercourse, by genital-to-genital contact. Oral-genital contact can also spread venereal diseases. These diseases can have grave consequences. Infections of the reproductive organs can make young people sterile and make it impossible for them to be parents.

Question: How far can you go before it is considered going too far?

Answer: I believe any time a girl allows a young man to touch her breasts or genital area, they have gone too far. Or if a girl touches a young man's genitals, they have gone too far. Petting increases sexual arousal, and all too frequently this leads to sexual intercourse and to guilt and disappointment.

Question: Should you kiss on the first date?

Answer: A kiss should be something special for someone special. There might be a rare occasion for a kiss on the first date, but generally it should be reserved only for someone important to you. The fact that you have gone out together does not mean you should kiss.

Question: Is it wrong to feel strong sexual desires for someone?

Answer: It is natural for young people to feel sexual desires. This is part of sexual development. But such feelings should be a sign to be cautious and to avoid necking and petting that could increase these desires greatly. Most young people who have had premarital sexual intercourse describe a sudden and almost total loss of control because of the intensity of their sexual emotions from heavy petting. All judgment and control was lost until it was too late. Then followed immediate regret. Sex is a God-given power. If we use it righteously and keep the commandments, we will have that power in the life to come. If we misuse it, it will be taken from us.

Question: Why do young men get sexually excited so quickly?

Answer: First, the male genital organs are external

and are therefore easily stimulated by even the slightest touch. The male hormone, testosterone, stimulates much of the daring and aggressive behavior of many young men. It also stimulates sexual aggression. Young men as well as young women are responsible for their conduct at all times, and they are especially responsible to control their sexual feelings *before* they become intense.

# Index

Abortion, 36
Accuracy important in teaching, 15, 49
Activity to counteract negative feelings, 48, 52
Adolescence stage, 17, 20-21, 51. *See also* Teenagers, teaching
Answering questions, 17-21. *See also* Responses to questions and situations
Availability of parents, 5

Babies. *See* Pregnancy
Bad words, children using, 28-30
Bath time, 24, 34-35
Bathing suit, 35
"Big night" method, 9-11
Bishop, 44, 53
Bleeding, explaining, 26-28
Books on sexuality, using, 11-12
Breast-feeding, 25-26, 35

Carefulness in conveying attitudes, 14-17
Cesarean section, 25
Chastity, law of, 37-38, 41
Children: learn about their sexuality naturally, 1-2, 21; can be taught by parents, 3-6; incorrect methods in teaching, 7-12; best method in teaching, 13-21; when to teach, 22-30; teaching principles and facts to, 31-39; as teenagers, 40-49, 52-55; never too late to teach, 50-51
Communication: increasing difficulty in, 8-9, 19-20, 40; establishing base for, 18-19, 21, 30; through questions and answers, 22-23, 52-55; through responses to situations, 24-29; between parents and teens, 40-46
Confession, 44, 53
Contraception, 33
Control. *See* Self-control
Courtship, 17, 20-21

Dating, 8, 20-21, 42-46
Development of child, 17-21
Differences, sexual, 18-19, 35-36
Diligence, 14-15, 17
Directness, 14-16, 20-21, 41-43, 49

Education, sexual: limitations of, in schools, 1-2, 5-6, 31; forfeiting control over, 9; is not isolated event, 10-11; in context of

# INDEX